T0012484

CONTENTS

Chapter 1

THE PRESSURE'S ON

AUGUST 9, 2016
RIO DE JANEIRO, BRAZIL

Simone Biles leaps and **tumbles** as she performs her **floor** routine in the team competition at the Olympics.

AMAZING MOMENTS IN SPORTS

SOARING to Gold!

Simone Biles at the 2016 Summer Olympics

By James Buckley Jr.
Illustrated by Tom Rogers

BEARPORT
PUBLISHING

Minneapolis, Minnesota

Credits

Cover art by Tom Rogers. Photos: 21 top: © AP Photos/Yomiuri Shimbun. 21 bottom: © Valeria Cantone/ Dreamstime.com. 22: © AP Photos/Suzanne Vlamis. 23: © Sasha Samardzjia/Dreamstime.com.

Bearport Publishing Company Product Development Team
President: Jen Jenson; Director of Product Development: Spencer Brinker; Managing Editor: Allison Juda; Associate Editor: Naomi Reich; Senior Designer: Colin O'Dea; Associate Designer: Elena Klinkner; Associate Designer: Kayla Eggert; Product Development Specialist: Anita Stasson

Produced by Shoreline Publishing Group LLC
Santa Barbara, California
Designer: Patty Kelley
Editorial Director: James Buckley Jr.

DISCLAIMER: This graphic story is a dramatization based on true events. It is intended to give the reader a sense of the narrative rather than a presentation of actual details as they occurred.

Library of Congress Cataloging-in-Publication Data

Names: Buckley, James, Jr., 1963- author. | Rogers, Tom (Illustrator)
   illustrator.
Title: Soaring to gold! : Simone Biles at the 2016 Summer Olympics / by
   James Buckley Jr. ; illustrated by Tom Rogers.
Description: Minneapolis, MN : Bearport Publishing Company, [2024] |
   Series: Amazing moments in sports | Includes bibliographical references
   and index.
Identifiers: LCCN 2023005602 (print) | LCCN 2023005603 (ebook) | ISBN
   9798885099929 (library binding) | ISBN 9798888221747 (paperback) | ISBN
   9798888223079 (ebook)
Subjects: LCSH: Biles, Simone, 1997---Juvenile literature. | Olympic Games
   (31st : 2016 : Rio de Janeiro, Brazil)--Juvenile literature. | Women
   gymnasts--United States--Biography. | Women Olympic athletes--United
   States--Biography.
Classification: LCC GV460.2.B55 B833 2024 (print) | LCC GV460.2.B55
   (ebook) | DDC 796.44092 [B]--dc23/eng/20230227
LC record available at https://lccn.loc.gov/2023005602
LC ebook record available at https://lccn.loc.gov/2023005603

For more information, write to Bearport Publishing, 5357 Penn Avenue South, Minneapolis, MN 55419.

Already a world champion, Simone came into the Olympics favored to win. But the question remained... could she do it with the whole world watching?

Simone grew up in Texas. She was a very active kid!

LOOK AT ME!

LOOKING GOOD, SIMONE!

When Simone was six, she went to watch some gymnasts practice.

WOW! THAT LOOKS LIKE FUN! I WANT TO DO THAT!

Simone was a natural from the start.

WHEW! I'M GLAD MY ACTIVE LITTLE SIMONE FOUND SOMETHING SHE LOVES TO DO!

WHEEE!

SHE'S PICKING IT UP QUICKLY. I BET SHE COULD BE REALLY GOOD!

Soon, Simone was finding herself on top of the winner's **podium**.

When she was 14, she won her first state **all-around** title.

And she didn't stop there.

2013 U.S. NATIONAL CHAMPIONSHIPS FOUR EVENT SILVERS AND ALL-AROUND GOLD

2013 WORLD CHAMPIONSHIP WORLD ALL-AROUND

2014 WORLD CHAMPIONSHIP **INDIVIDUAL** ALL-AROUND, TEAM GOLD, AND TWO EVENT GOLDS

2015 WORLD CHAMPIONSHIP SIMONE IS FIRST EVER TO WIN THREE STRAIGHT ALL-AROUND TITLES

Although she was **dominating** her sport, Simone hadn't yet earned the biggest prize in gymnastics—gold at the Olympic Games. For that, she headed to Rio de Janeiro.

WELCOME TO RIO!

LET'S GO FOR THE GOLD!

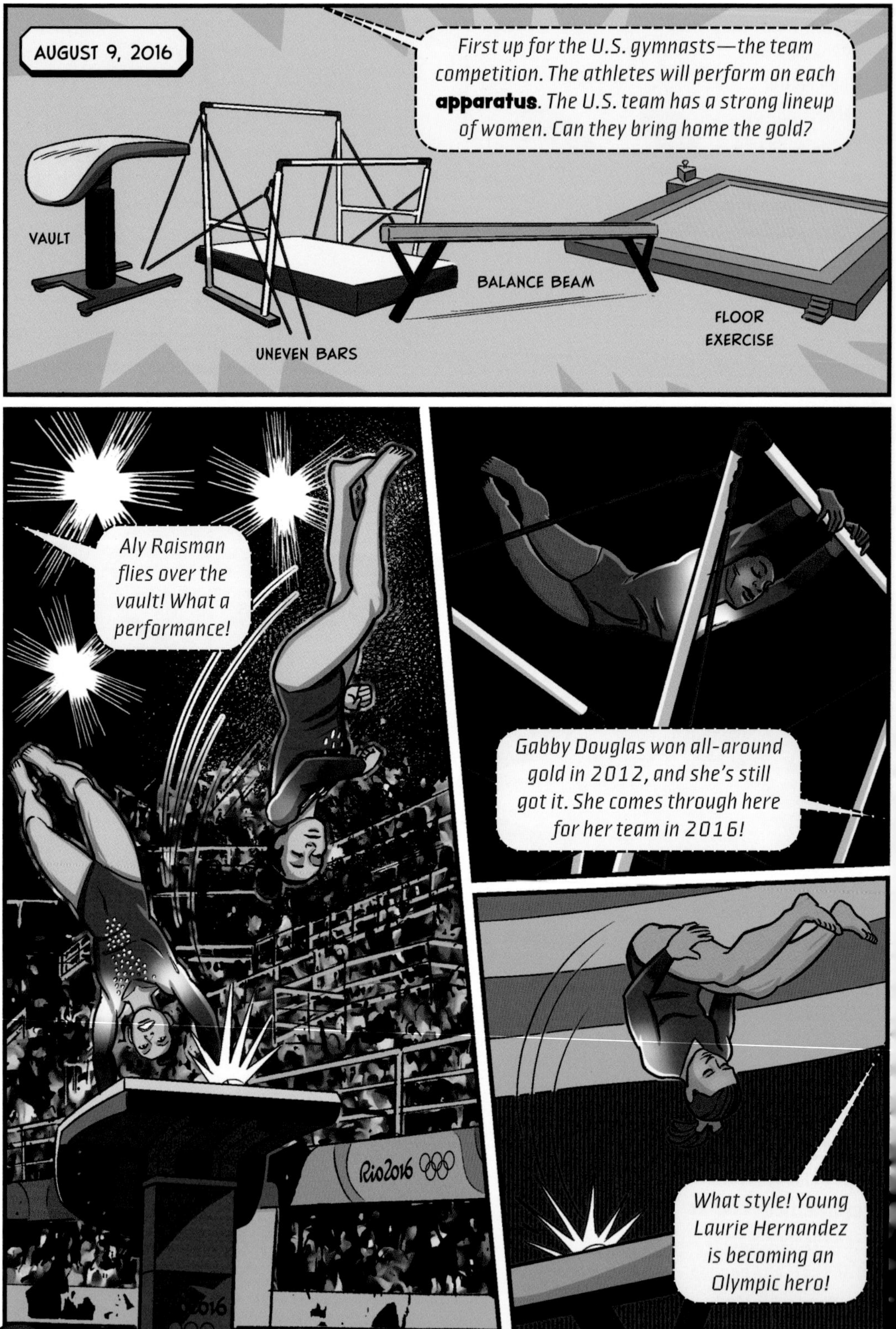
AUGUST 9, 2016
First up for the U.S. gymnasts—the team competition. The athletes will perform on each **apparatus**. The U.S. team has a strong lineup of women. Can they bring home the gold?
VAULT
UNEVEN BARS
BALANCE BEAM
FLOOR EXERCISE
Aly Raisman flies over the vault! What a performance!
Rio2016
Gabby Douglas won all-around gold in 2012, and she's still got it. She comes through here for her team in 2016!
What style! Young Laurie Hernandez is becoming an Olympic hero!

The American women proudly wore their gold medals from the team event.

But the Olympics were not over. For Simone, there was even more to come!

Chapter 2
SIMONE SOARS!

Rio2016

AUGUST 11, 2016

Please welcome the athletes for the women's all-around final! Each gymnast will perform on all four apparatuses. The top total score wins the gold!

Simone began with the vault. Her score of 15.866 was the highest of everyone!

HERE WE GO!

Rio2016

The bars were not Simone's strongest event. Her score was only seventh best.

Another top score for Simone, this time on the balance beam—one of her specialties!

The last event was the floor exercise. Simone blew away the competition here, too!

At the end of the day, Simone was named the winner!

She got her second gold medal of the Olympics!

SIMONE, YOU DID IT! WE'RE SO PROUD!

YOU HAD TO DEAL WITH A LOT OF PRESSURE, AND YOU CAME THROUGH!

THANKS!

AUGUST 14, 2016

Simone had won gold in both of the competitions so far. But she had a chance for more in three individual event finals. A champion would be crowned in each.

The first individual event was the vault. Simone put up the highest score!

Another gold for Simone!

Simone got a bronze medal on beam.

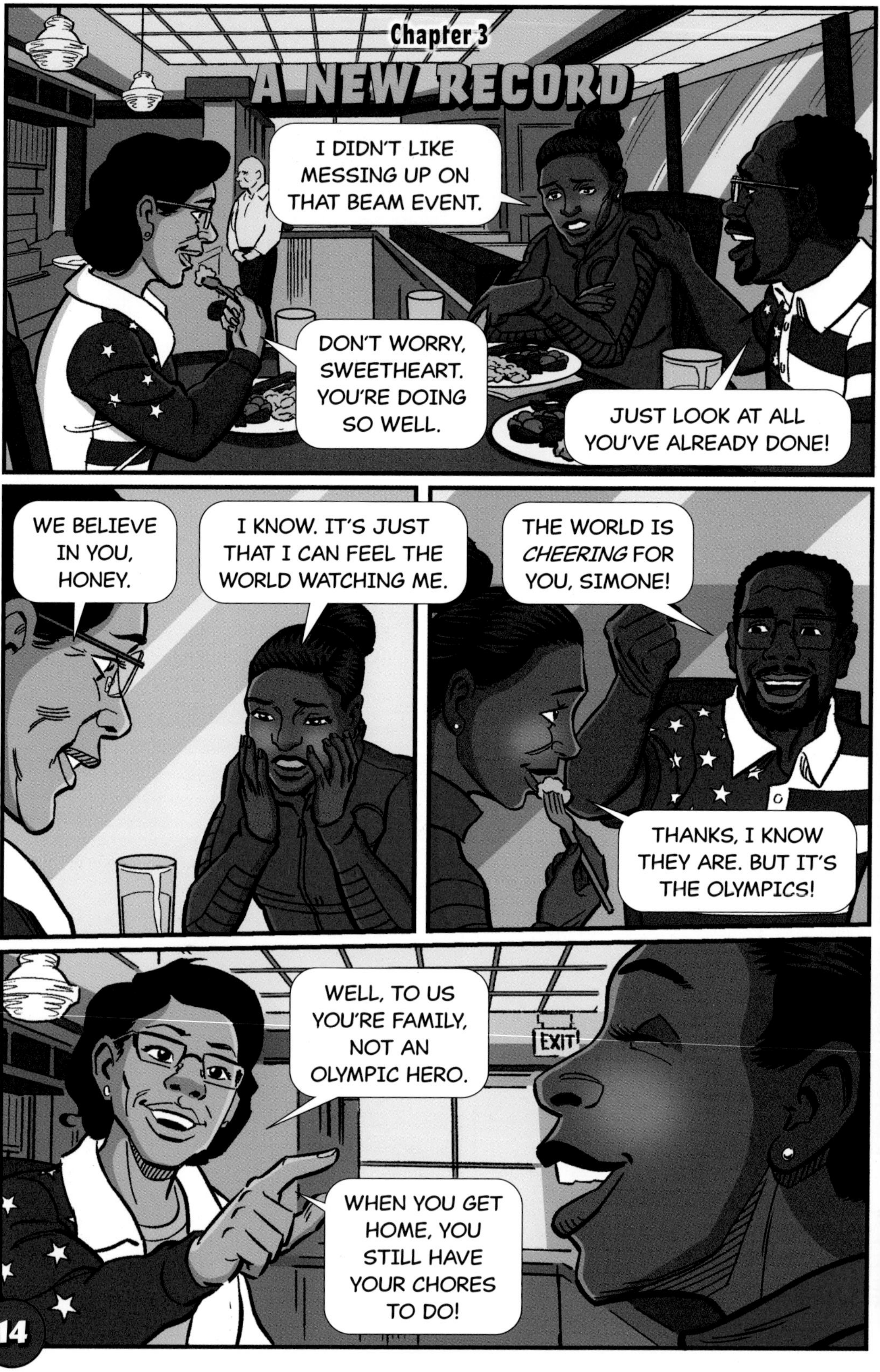
Chapter 3
A NEW RECORD
I DIDN'T LIKE MESSING UP ON THAT BEAM EVENT.
DON'T WORRY, SWEETHEART. YOU'RE DOING SO WELL.
JUST LOOK AT ALL YOU'VE ALREADY DONE!
WE BELIEVE IN YOU, HONEY.
I KNOW. IT'S JUST THAT I CAN FEEL THE WORLD WATCHING ME.
THE WORLD IS *CHEERING* FOR YOU, SIMONE!
THANKS, I KNOW THEY ARE. BUT IT'S THE OLYMPICS!
WELL, TO US YOU'RE FAMILY, NOT AN OLYMPIC HERO.
EXIT
WHEN YOU GET HOME, YOU STILL HAVE YOUR CHORES TO DO!

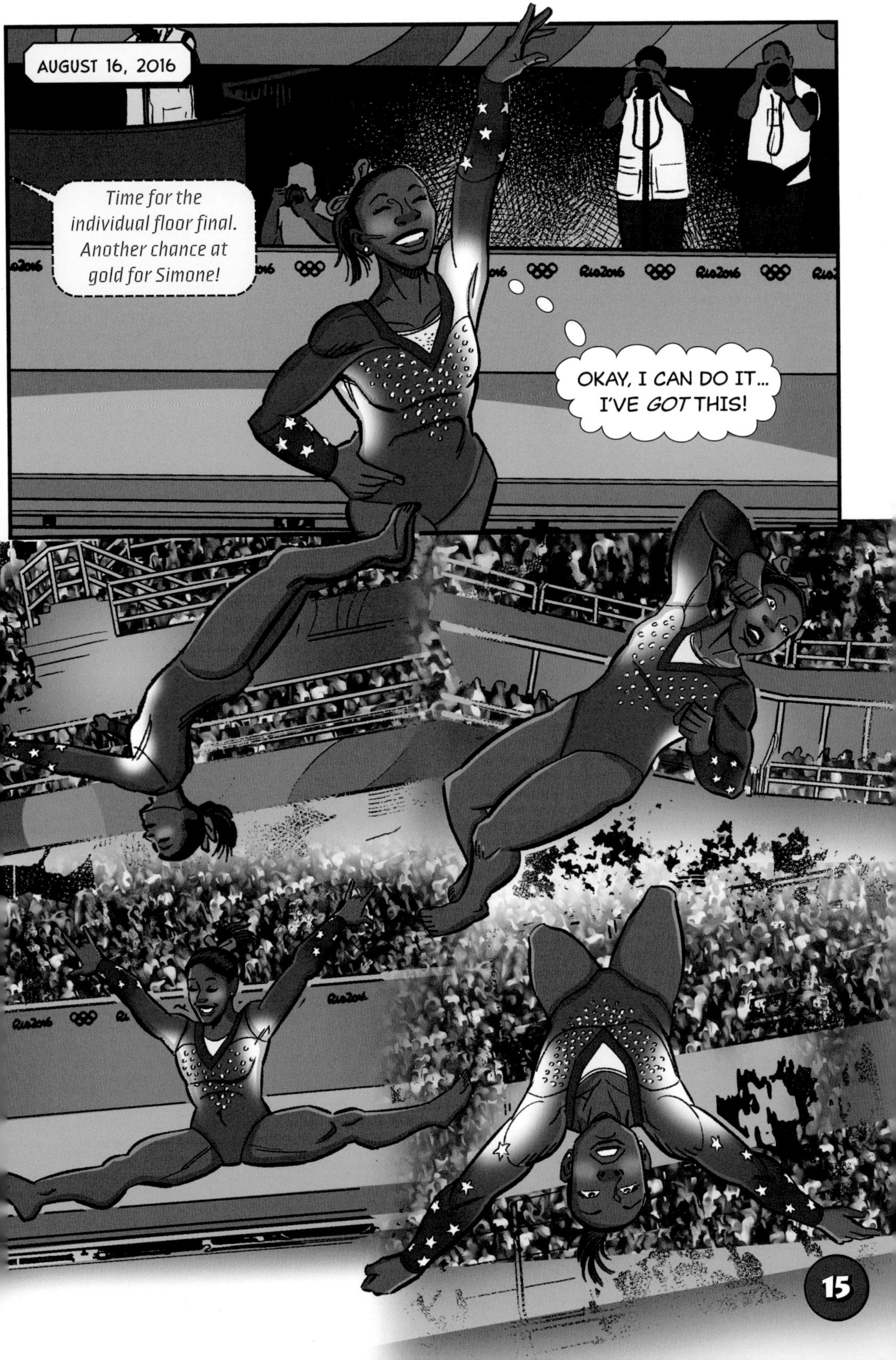
AUGUST 16, 2016
Time for the individual floor final. Another chance at gold for Simone!
OKAY, I CAN DO IT... I'VE *GOT* THIS!
Rio2016

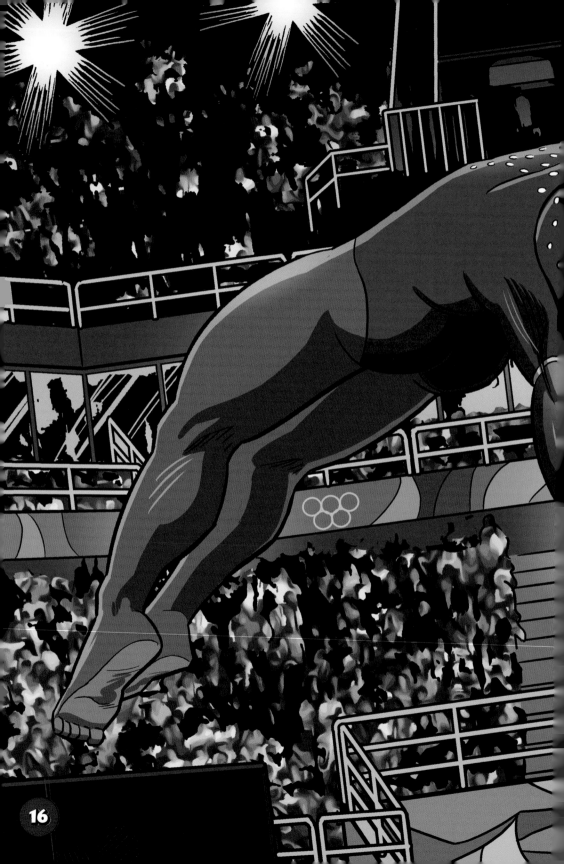

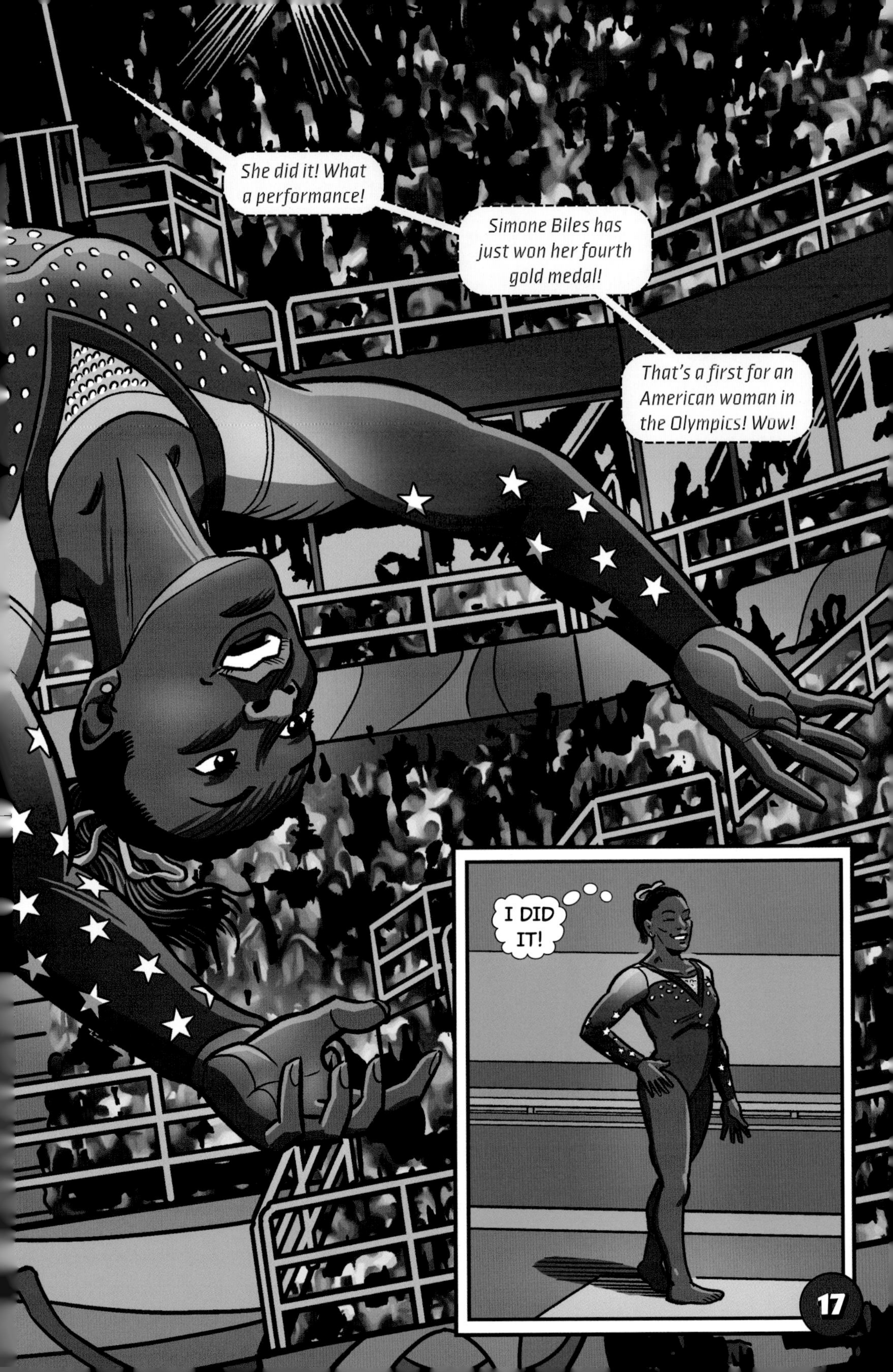
She did it! What a performance!
Simone Biles has just won her fourth gold medal!
That's a first for an American woman in the Olympics! Wow!
I DID IT!

Simone was the biggest star at the Rio Olympics!

Her amazing success and winning personality led the U.S. team to choose her as the flag-bearer for the Olympic closing ceremonies. It was one more huge honor for this hero!

Simone's four golds helped the U.S. women's gymnastics team have their most successful Olympics ever!

Simone became a real role model. She continued to work hard, winning more medals and championships.

She also made the brave choice not to compete when she wasn't in the right mental space. Simone spoke out in support of mental health in sports.

In 2022, her gymnastics success and work helping others brought her to the White House. Simone became the youngest person ever to receive the Presidential Medal of Freedom!

19

OLYMPIC GYMNASTICS HISTORY

Women's gymnastics has been part of the Summer Olympic Games since 1928. It has grown to be one of the most popular sports of the Games. Women compete on four apparatuses individually along with all-around competitions as part of the artistic gymnastics events.

- Larisa Latynina of the Soviet Union has won the most women's gymnastics medals, with 18 (9 gold, 5 silver, and 4 bronze) over the course of 3 Olympics (1956, 1960, and 1964).

- Simone Biles and Shannon Miller are tied for the most medals among American women, with seven each.

- The Soviet Union won a record nine team gold medals, all from 1952 to 1988.

- Beginning in 1984, **rhythmic** gymnastics was added to the Olympics. In that sport, athletes combine tumbling moves on a mat with throwing and catching clubs, a ball, or a ribbon on a stick.

- Trampoline gymnastics became an Olympic sport in 2000. Gymnasts soar high into the air above a bouncy, canvas trampoline, performing mid-air flips and spins.

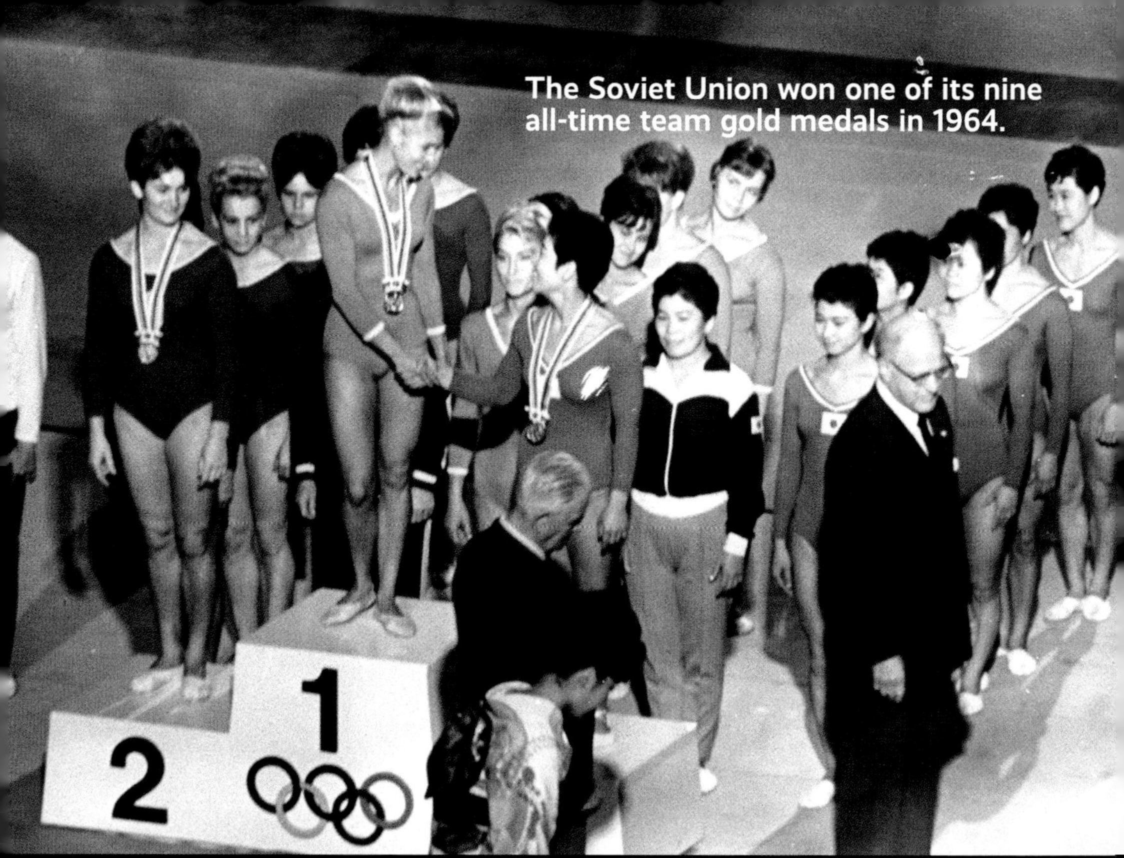
2
1

The Soviet Union won one of its nine all-time team gold medals in 1964.

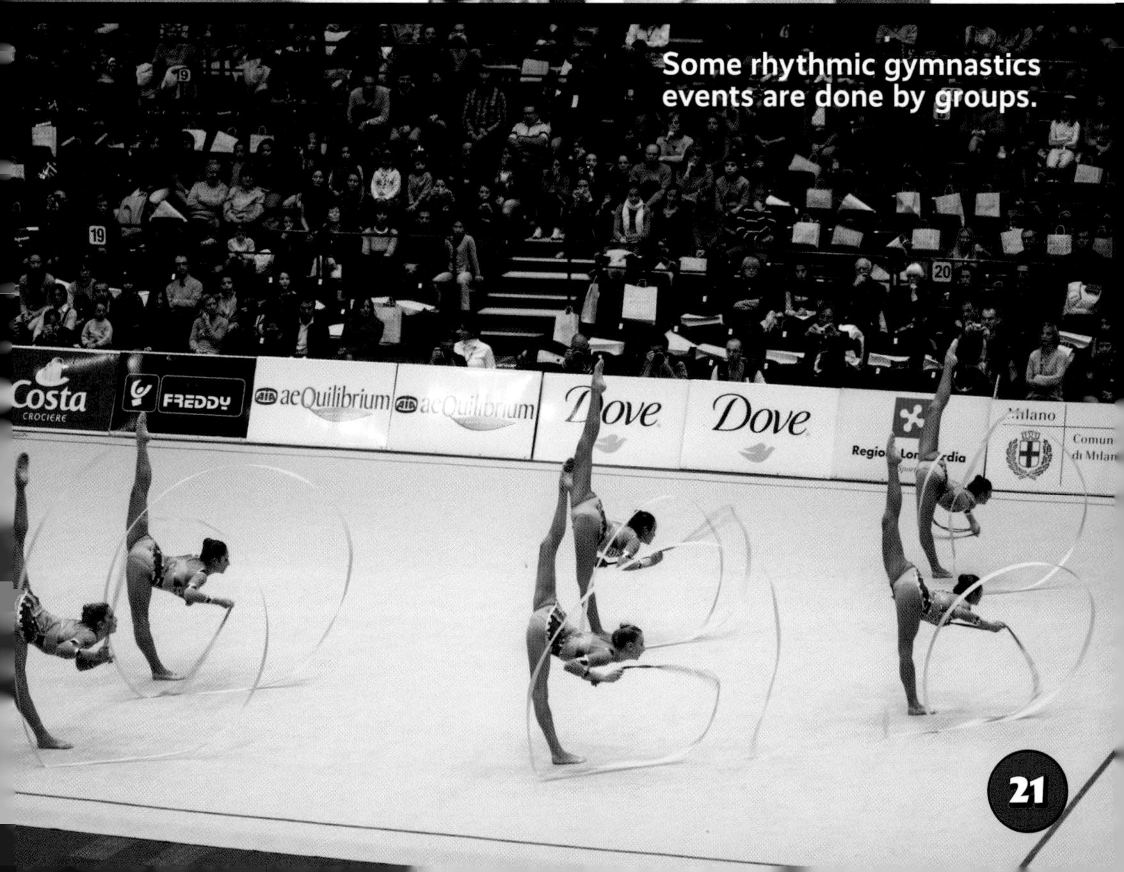
Costa
CROCIERE
FREDDY
aeQuilibrium
Dove
Dove

Some rhythmic gymnastics events are done by groups.

OTHER GYMNASTICS STARS

Nadia Comaneci was a Romanian star who, in 1976, became the first gymnast ever to earn a 10. She achieved the perfect score on the uneven bars and went on to score six more 10s as she piled up three gold medals. She added two more golds in 1980.

Mary Lou Retton won the all-around gold during the 1984 Olympics in Los Angeles, earning two perfect 10s along the way. She was the first woman from the United States to win the all-around title. She also won four other medals at the same Olympic Games.

Gabby Douglas was the first person of color to win the Olympic all-around gold medal, which she earned in 2012. She also helped the U.S. team win a surprise gold medal in the team event at those same Olympics.

Mary Lou Retton was the star of the 1984 Games.

GLOSSARY

all-around a gymnastics event in which athletes compete in all areas of the sport

apparatus the equipment used for an event

dominating taking over or winning by a large amount

floor the gymnastic event in which athletes tumble, flip, and dance on a soft mat

individual alone, by oneself

podium a platform with several levels on which sports champions receive their awards

rhythmic a kind of gymnastics in which the gymnast uses ribbons, hoops, or other equipment

tumbles moves on a mat in a way that includes somersaults, flips, rolls, and handstands

INDEX

READ MORE

Burk, Rachelle. *The Story of Simone Biles.* Emeryville, CA: Rockridge Press, 2020.

Loh, Stefanie. *Who Is Simone Biles?* New York: Penguin Workshop, 2023.

Nicholson, Tracy. *Unbelievable Stories of Simone Biles.* Sheridan, Wyoming: Kids Castle Press, 2021.

LEARN MORE ONLINE

1. Go to **www.factsurfer.com** or scan the QR code below.
2. Enter **"Soaring to Gold"** into the search box.
3. Click on the cover of this book to see a list of websites.